I0163859

An Impaired Love: A Pickup Artist's Handbook.

& Commentary on Religious Dualities in the Text of AIL.

By Jay Irish

ISBN-13:
978-0692489093 (AN IMPAIRED LOVE LLC)

ISBN-10:
0692489096

Jay Ireys
P.O. Box 445
Clinton, IN 47842
Jaireys@hushmail.com

A Study Guide and Pickup Artist's Handbook to
Accompany *An Impaired Love.*

by Jay Ireys.

Contents

FORWORD

This book is going to make you popular, almost too popular, so be careful as you deal with its subject matter. Going into this it may be easy to think this material won't help you get women, that its just not going to happen, but trust me it will and if you act like it isn't it will just make it worse. This book is not written by a pickup artist who went to the bars every night trying to learn how to pick up drunk chicks.

The material you find in this book is written by a guy who met girls at all hours of the day, or night, and went from being a nobody to a local legend. Granted a lot of the time girls were there looking for sex, but more times than not these girls were approached sober and just trying to have a good time. The methods inside this book are complex, but not in practice.

The time it takes for you to think about the material presented within is the time it takes to score with the ladies. Good luck on your journey to legend status, just follow the material and try to keep an open mind.

There are a lot of NLP, Self-help, hypnotism,

and psychology hints in the material- but I assure you that just because this book is presented in more of a study format that doesn't mean you won't be prepared to pick up chicks and to be hit on by hot women.

The real secrets in this book are encoded in the stories of three individuals, but don't worry each story is broken down into its component parts, and afterwards there is good discussion on the underlying principles of why these tactics are so effective- and they are effective.

This study on An Impaired Love was completed through extensive and comprehensive cross checking between the text of AIL and the Christian Bible. All pertinent sections of the previous written material were analyzed and compared extensively for both passages, words, and the origins of these words. The resulting text is contained in this study guide as a companion to AIL. The text is meant for the serious reader or the initiate with questions concerning the inherent philosophy contained in the text of AIL.

As of right now you have 'Game'

I was never the awkward kid that never got girls, at first. At first, I was the aggressive kid who just took whatever he wanted and got away with it just fine. The problem I encountered was that as my tastes in women grew I started packing on baggage. Now please understand I don't mean anything bad by saying baggage, its just that the more women I picked up the more guy friends started to follow along- the problem was I wasn't a guru and had no time to even consider that these guys wanted help with the ladies. I never considered they wanted help, so what did I do? I mistakenly started taking advice from some so called pick up artists and I transferred this info to the rear, I started packing baggage just like the average pick up artist is bound to do.

The main focus of my energies in teaching you these methods comes from a sort of empathy for my readers. To explain I must remind the reader that I was very popular from the get go, it was just that I quickly got bogged down by the world. The tricks and methods I give here are based a lot on being natural, but more-so on what works in the real world, and how to effectively perform, or out-perform, all of the competition.

When it comes down to what makes a real pick up artist, or any playboy for that matter, the secret is just as I will divulge it. The 90-10 rule applies- even though the game is 90 percent of just being your own true alpha self, its the ten percent that counts. These 10% are what I learned after getting the girls, and what eventually led to my picking up the most beautiful women, women I didn't even know that flocked to my door.

The Big 3

Have you ever heard the story about the three goats trying to cross over a bridge that has a troll living underneath it

Love can be like this to an extent. You might be able to get away with a few little things and you might be able to let others get away with some of the little things, but the big things always get noticed.

If you really want to practice the effects and methods of this book, then you need to realize that a book cannot make up the right conditions necessary for you to get what you want, you have to do this. Nothing in this book is designed to create environments in which you have control-

This is what you have to do. You have to go out and do the little things before you can get noticed in a big way. That's what this book is designed to do- Get noticed in a big way!

By getting noticed immediately for your pick up game or your skills with women, you limit yourself to what you'll be able to do when you're really ready. Instead of trying to sleep with women immediately, you need to treat this like the three Billy goats- start small and cross each bridge that you come to, but don't forget to invest in yourself and any possible reputation that might come your way because reputation will be key in getting strangers to offer you their sex.

It's important to always be prepared for success. The preparation you receive in this book is not just tips for you to follow, but actual ways to delve into the worlds you want to be in. I say worlds, but maybe the word 'places' is more apt. You don't have to go to a bar to pick up women, or a club. Granted a lot of women who want sex frequent these locals, but you don't need that per say. With these methods if you try them recklessly, you might end up with multiple women at one time. So, be careful.

What love?

While it's true that I cannot make this book to make you do anything, it is possible in making this book to use techniques on my end that will enhance the way in which you perform the methods on you end. NLP, hypnosis, self-help; all of these things are great but the most effective technique I have ever learned was taught to me in college as I earned my English degree.

This technique promised that by simple writing, and thus a reader, I would be completely able to tap into the psyche of any individual and communicate with the genetic whole of that person. Imagine by using simple commonalities and archetypes, especially certain doctrines and symbols, that you can communicate over the internet, or by pen and paper, between individuals in a way as complex as any geneticist in the laboratory.

The secret is that time is eternal, and for what that's worth, we all have the cave-man, - alpha-male living inside us just as much as we have the star-dwelling-future-man waiting for us. Getting to both of these alternate personas is what's important, as well as getting to the opposite sexes. To become an instant legend in your town, city, state it is important that you do your own research as well. Just for the reason that you have a chance encounter with another living being that also knows these techniques you should know what's behind your new game. Luckily, the first person to use this game was dead a long time ago, so no one person can actually claim it as their own. Why its been kept a secret for so long is anybody's guess, but I'd put my money on the fact that it not only gets sex from women, but it earns love and trust- by the way of perfect 10 sex.

And that's the 10% from the rule we talked about earlier. Its being the perfect lover. The one the women want so bad they talk about when no guys are around. Just don't get a complex after it happens to you, but be ready for one.

If this sounds interesting to you, and is something you really know you want- then just keep reading!

CHAPTER ONE
An Impaired Love

Dragons wear tanned leather jackets, or thick wool, and they look good; they fascinate. Wherever they go they are loved, never hated; even when alone they emit love like fire. They carry goods in their pockets: money and death; and they travel with the lions at times, but are ever mighty just the same. At home, or indoors wherever they are, they are naked and pale, and constantly wailing shrill cries. Others that come near them dare not come to close, for they fear them and are deafened by the Dragons roars, wailings and the sharp tongues that cut into the ears of those that come near. Dare they come into calling range these others become afraid and fall silent; enemies lose heart in the presence of the Dragons, and they become heavy inn their limbs and lame, their minds become frantic and wild, they shudder and stoop, and then turn away in go in disbelief.

Friends come like messengers to the dens of the Dragons. There the wailings make these fellows draw near, only to fall back at the will of the Dragons, or to fall at the touch of the thick leather coats, the skins of the Dragons. Only these divine friends may see the Dragons in a close proximity, naked and beautiful. They are enlightened momentarily in delight when in the presence of the Dragon. Dragons receive the messengers only in the day, for it is light. The message of the Dragons returns to the Dragons at night, resting near their heads. Only when a message does not return does it fall flat, and mute, the messenger goes blind and the Dragon must go to the place the message died, and there receive it, and revive it. The Dragon may punish the messenger only in that place the dead message was found, or the Dragon may take the fallen messenger to a place of other fallen messengers, and messages, and the like, a mass of darkness for which many Dragons will come to walk among the, and in the midst of them

A mass of Dragons may allow for new Dragons to don jackets, or skins as they are known. Skins which when worn are beautiful, tanned and wide, and those that wear them are now the new Dragons, whom will wear the name of the Dragon. From this meeting many more Dragons will arise, and they too will prosper and share in drinking and reveling as the new sons to a wide family. Only those messengers that kept fear of the Dragons, and kept the message alive, will be named anew, and remembered, partying with the Dragons. In time, these new dragons too will be alike and have messengers come to them, and these new messengers shall be comforted and walk in the light of the Dragons, the eternal fire of them that are luminous in the day, and those that do come to see them will and all like them shall learn messages, and be affected by the light; then becoming like light and bearing light away they become messages in the day, yet those that are not of good accord and spirit, and such, fear and stumble in the fire, and burn up. These will not join the Dragons, but be cast down instead to that level of the pitiful and base of mind- never to look upon them that do their part, them then having knowledge only of the night.

Dragons carry a name, and a message, and a likeness to each other so that their messages become like sound to those around, and in this like sound the fire consumes and changes becoming one, yet still separate and alike. Those alike and those not alike will be different and yet still one; and as one, and as one of them, and one in likeness to them all and to the fire of them- one shall be one to emanate life and to the world what they will. This will being theirs alone, alike and not alike, being that of those that pursue, those that perish, and those that proceed; also those that fall away only to become at rest by the revived at the great gatherings of the masses of the Dragons, to be looked upon by all and to fall below their eyes.

Those that perish and them that fall away being without fear, will be brought back in darkness and they will be of hard speech, yet all coming to form the brightness of fire; they too may again be seen to walk in the clouded days until that time they are called back together with all like them, and not knowing which will be next to be lifted up and breathed upon by the Dragons- initiated to live among the Dragons forever; initiated to issue the next message, the next message of light and fire. May the good men be good messengers who carry good messages, knowing no evil, and being true while carrying the light to others to whom need be; to receive and be the next to come near to the den of light, to be the Divine protection and humility- to become that prodigal son that cast a good shadow in coming into sight of the Dragons.

One-Night

"From the first time I saw her I knew she was going to be mine." This is what I thought about as   he sat next to her on my couch, in my apartment. She was right at home sitting with him on the sofa facing the T.V. as I played v-jay for over an hour. I felt like a clown trying to entertain them just wishing he would leave, but I needed him to be there because I couldn't figure out just how to get her to sleep with me, and I knew he could sleep with her that night.

My plan in bringing him here was to get him to loosen up drinking a few beers, while I stayed sober enough to notice how it was that he got so close to her so fast. It worked of course because five minutes after he arrived she was next to him getting closer and closer with him, just giggling like a schoolgirl and laughing every time he said her name.

After an hour of watching them together while I played cool video after video, I started to feel tired. I could have given up like I usually do and just told them to leave. But what good would that of done because if I did that he was sure to sleep with her that night- and that's what I wanted to do. So instead of telling them I was tired and just giving it up and letting her walk off with him I changed gears. I started playing the same videos over and over. I started playing the videos nobody likes- not even me. And before long his game started to give way.

I had introduced a little bit of awkwardness to the room, and their conversation started to give, which is just what I needed for an opening. I took the insults and dirty looks with a grain of salt and started playing the good videos, the ones we hadn't seen yet, but not before I was sitting in front of the two of them with their sole attention now on me.

You see, they had to take a breath before commencing the flirting anymore, mostly to spare each other the embarrassment of what had happened on the T.V. Well I took that opportunity to sit down in front of them and start suggesting some of the videos were really awesome, the ones I played while they were too busy staring into each other's eyes. They had no choice but to agree, and here's why:

They didn't know each other well enough to assume they had so much in common so that they could sit together for an hour and cozy up to one another. They needed me in the background making things look great, playing all the latest and greatest videos of their lives so that they could talk, baby talk. Once I made the videos awkward the two of them had to back up, they were feeling awkward to, so I gave myself the chance to come over and sit right in front of the T.V.

Neither of them cared too much about the T.V. though so they had to just sit and wait for something to come up for them to baby talk about. I didn't give them that chance though, instead I sat there and talked about the videos, and not to him either- but to her. She took every word I said about the videos as good as gold for a number of reasons:

1. She had already gave her opinions on most of them to him, but now she was sitting with me and had to repeat her voice.

2. I knew her better than he did because I had been listening to her and he had only been trying to use a routine to keep the baby talk going.

3. I played the videos so I knew more about them than he ever could have.

After I began a conversation with the girl the night went much more the way I had wanted it. The only problem was now that I had shut down my drunken friend he was turning into a bit of a problem for me. I couldn't get rid of him just yet because he had turned into the entertainment for the night, now that I was done playing v-j.

He copped an attitude pretty quick, so I had to move him to the kitchen with the beer, while I took his seat at the couch, with her. I knew he would have to regroup and try to gain command of his game before returning, which he did but by that time it was too late. You see, I wasn't drinking so I had my wits and finesse when it came to the physical act I laid on my new girlfriend at the couch. He sat on the floor in front of us, but in a matter of minutes he was on his back beer in hand. I had my arm around her, and suggested we move to the bedroom, which we did- we left him lying there, and I told him to let himself out when he was finished laying there. I scored. Not him.

I took her into the bedroom and the next time I came out of there he was no longer hanging around. He apparently got the point and the next time I spoke with him he wanted to know what had happened to that beautiful girl. He asked this thinking I had let her get away, and thus caused him to miss his big chance with her, but that's not what happened as I explained to him. He couldn't believe it when I told him what did happen and tried to put it off as a fluke in his game, but I know better- I had completely destroyed his tried and proved game, one that he had polished off on every living person he knew. And what did I do- I used a completely unheard of technique that caused this girl to love me, as I will explain in the next sections.

Recap

1. How do you say her name? Does it sound stern and authoritative? Or does it sound friendly and warming? Have you ever heard the pick-up lines that go with a girl's name? Here are a few you need to get to know.

-You look like a Cindy?

-Hey have we met, what's your name again?

-God, J----, I know we just met but it feels like I have known you forever, like maybe in a past life, or something.

Do these sound familiar to you? They should because they're in the movies, on T.V., and in all the best literature. Someone always seems to make a big deal out of a person's name, but why? The answer is pretty simple, its because they have to build strong rapport with the girl as fast as possible, and saying her name is the number one way to do this. So its true what they say about it all being in a name. Not that that means you need to know everyone's name before you sleep with them, but only that if you do chose to use her name you need to be 100% sure you can say it in a friendly, comfortable manner.

2. Know your stuff. If you are going to memorize anything that resembles a routine to pick up women, don't waste your time. Use your time wisely and memorize specific facts and popular nuances, so that way when you actually do talk to a women she won't feel like you are wasting her time- like so many others.

Example: You hear a song in a public place while standing next to a group. The hottest female in the group says she loves the song. The alpha male of the group has no choice but to say he too also loves the song. You can now feel safe in saying to the group I know this song its "G--", and by telling them the facts you know you become instantly more interesting than them- so much so that they want to be around you.

3. It wasn't so much that I wanted to have the best time that night. I just wanted to sleep with this girl, not that she was anyone in particular, just a girl I wanted to sleep with. I didn't need to be the

life of the party or extremely social, I just needed to be driven.

It could have happened the other way around with me letting myself out of my own apartment, but it didn't because I was prepared. I knew exactly what to do and when to do it, so much more than my pick up artist friend whom by the way sticks to the numbers, the game plan, just a little too much for his own good. Playing by the number is the number one way to lose- and that goes for any situation in life.

Drama 101

If you can get a woman's name and use it correctly, in a warm, confident, and friendly manner you are half way there.

If you can use your own specific knowledge of important and relevant things you can get all the way there.

If Love is what you want, all you have to do is find it. It should stick out in the real world, every opportunity to find Love, it should be obvious. All you have to do is to find the thing, this would preferably be a women, and learn its name. After that all you have to do is keep exercising that name on your tongue and trying it around new and exciting people and things.

The real secret is in what you say and how you say it. You don't need a routine, but if you want to get good at using names try reading those books they sell in the grocery stores that list all the most popular baby names and what each name means. This is great exercise and will pay off the first time there is a name you recognize and need to use.

The thing to do in speaking is to match your partner in tone, in timing, and in registry. What I mean is you need to speak at the same volume as her. You can't be too loud all the time, its a turn off that makes it look like you can't hear. You need to keep your attention focused on the moment. Girls love this, and its more fun, so don't try to act.

Pay attention to her and try to keep up, if she is ready for sex that means she's getting excited in a certain way, you need to feed into this and if she starts to laugh or giggle at your jokes then need to stop joking and laugh a little too to show her your still paying attention.

When you talk to her make sure your talking to her. In the first few minutes of any conversation I try to win her over, but as soon as you see this working you need to move your speech and attention away from winning the room to winning her. Move in close and start to speak more directly to and about her, and pay attention- and don't forget her name.

In order to speak to the woman inside the woman, which is the woman you want to speak to, you have to be the man that women want to be with. By releasing your inner alpha-male she must respond in kind, or she's not worth the time. By using this method of speech and attention you are reaching her inner woman, that's the one that wants you, it'll work every time if you let it.

Ch.1 Notes

Malachi; tannah; tanniyn; drakon; derkomai; Malachi 2-3; De. 32:33; Ps. 91:13; Is. 34.13; Je. 9:11; Mi. 1:8;

Malachi; charash; cherseh; kophos; kopto; temno; Mal. 2; Is.6:10; Je. 6:10; Eze. 12:2; Zec. 7:11; 2 Ti. 4:4; dullness; hardness; indifference; impenitence; unbelief;

Malachi3:1; Divine Messenger: Mt. 21:37; Jn. 6:38, 3:16; Messenger; malak; melakah; tsiyr; tsoor; tsiyr; aggelos; Mt. 21:37; Jn. 6:38, 7:29, 8:42, 9:4, 10:36, 17:8

Intercessor; paga; Lu. 23:24; Intercessory prayers; Ex. 32:32; 1 S. 7:5; 1Chr. 21:17

Malachi 3:16; Lu. 24:15; Saints Fellowship; chebar; tesumeth; yad; koinonia; koinonos; sun; metoche; sugkoinoneo; Lu. 24:15; Ac:42; Ro. 1:12; 1 Jn. 1:7

Ps 106:47

Malachi 4; Eternal Fire; owr; uwr; owrah; Uwriyel, Uriel; ale; phos; phosphoros;

Malachi 4:1; Re. 14:10; Re. 20:10; Re. 20:15, 21:8;

Jude 9-19; Micheal; Satan; Cain; Balaam; Korah; Enoch; Adam; God, A Judge; Christ, Judge; Apostles; Christ, Lord;

Jude 9; Miykael; Micheal; Satan; Satan; Da. 10:13; Re. 12:7; Ge. 3:14; Mt. 13:38; Mt. 13:39;

Jude 10-11; Qayin; Kain; Bilam; Balaam; Qorach: Kore; 1Jn. 3:12; Ge. 4:9; 2 Pe. 2:15; Nu. 16:1-3, 26:10;

Jude 12-15; Ge. 5:24; He. 11:1,3,5,6; chonowk; Enoch; adam;

Jude 16-19; Jude 1:19;

Jonah 1:4-8; Falsehood; maal; shaqaq; 1 Chr. 16:26; Is. 2:8; Je 2:11; Ga. 4:8; 1 Cor. 8:5;

Jonah 2:2-6; Preservation; Preserve; shamar; zoogoneo; Preserving the Faithful; De. 6:24; Ps. 31:23, 37:28; Pr 2:8; Is. 49:8; 2 Ti. 4:18

Divine Protection; 2 Chr. 16:9; Ps. 34:7, 91:4, 125:2; Zec 2:5; Lu. 21:18*; Ge. 35:5; Ex. 14:20; 2 K 6:17; Re. 7:3;

Jonah 3:6-10; Humility; anavah; tapeinophrosune; Prodigal Sun; Lu. 15:18

Jonah 4:4-8; tsalal; ts'latsol; kataskiazo; episkiazo; Divine Overshadowing;

Overshadowing Providence; Ex. 33:22; Is. 51:16; Apple of the Eye; Ps. 17:8

Spiritual Blindness; Is. 59:10; De. 33:27; Ps. 98:1; Re. 15:2

CHAPTER TWO
An Impaired Love

Delight in the day and night, for the way I will give you will break them in pieces. Serve with fear and trembling as if to kiss the sun but a little, but trust and increase least you be against me without help. Yes, be my shield and listen as I do; for I am not afraid of them around me. You will break the teeth of your enemy and will sit next to me with your own heart. My voice will you hear in the morning when you look up, and no evil will be there, and no fool will be in your sight.

Having destroyed those that speak deceit, come into my house and make way before me, forgetting those that flatter and all flattery of sorts; let them fall; call them out those rebels- shout for joy; yes, defend your love with you- come as a shield to me. I have seen the grief and made them to depart that have heard me; they are ashamed for in you I put my trust. Deliver me, so that they may not come like lions; arise and be an end to them, try the reins of my defenses. Keep heart and turn not away- for he wields a mighty sword.

Go and sing high and sing low, like an angel

with glory and honor- yet put out their name for ever- a refuge. Know your name for those that seek you out, and don't forget the humble- that I suffer of those that hate me, lift me up from the depths and I will rejoice in you- not being made to sink into a pit, a net made and hid- yet the makers own foot will be taken in the trap he has set, and so snared, turned to hell- so I am not always forgotten.

Don't let my expectation perish, nor let mean men prevail in your sight- still put fear into men, men that know never to be taken in the trap, the devices imagined through pride; those shadows. Walk, walk and speak, and protect me, for in you I trust, so prove my heart- I am purposed-"Keep me as the apple of the eye." Hide me under the shadow of your wings; their eyes cast down, like the lion lurking in secret places. When I awake I will see the likenesses of them I love. My recollection of favor, of grace- of love. Like a friend and giver my trusted prayer, my trusted confidant, my bold friend. Faithful and true in virtuous places- come and appoint me to stand and assure you of convictions held.

The gift of light comes from the sun to the earth; may the light appoint salvation to joyful living. Light from the heavens brighter than the star's radiance; each heart a candle in a burning house of hope and peace- our creation will be our loving gift to the night. We will raise up one from among us, and we will hear him according to our desires. We will hear him say, "Let us not hear again the voice nor see the great fire, least we die." We will agree with the one we raise up and be pleased for we put these words in his mouth, and he will speak them to all that come. He will speak our commandments, our blessings, and our warnings too, followed by our curses.

We will put a pot on the fire and watch it boil; then gathering into it all the good pieces and choice ones- then it will boil well and on the surface of the pot will be the scum; whose scum but our own, then bringing out every piece- may every piece be purged from filth, for I take away the desire of the eyes, yet not to see one cry. Make no tears at all, but bind your head fast upon you and put shoes on your feet, so that he that escapes may come to you and you and him together may be dumb no more, but become a sign to them. Our festivities have called for our fasts, our temperance will be our remedy, like oil to heroes. Death and hell are of man, and are man's final enemies; the revealers of our souls which will not be happy until justice is achieved. The just suffer too proving their innocence; they are just, yet are we- and so will we struggle as free, and of free men; and we must want to enjoy peace- Once pride is broken, renewed and the skies are darkened. Blood shed of our own is but a dishonor to the signs we prove, and are proved by.

Thus we depart and are called away yet again; letting our fruits fall to the ground, nature closes around us for a time and falseness endures; We arise, with new vigor, renewed- and life returns to the skies in light to the four points; as thought four angels to the four winds- the masters of virtue- That which is force, power, miracle and that which is believed to be the balancing of forces and movement with equilibrium. A great feast in which none came, and yet we were beholden in fear (for favor is deceitful) of that which came out of it, this feast whose only true guest was the host himself, and he whom sought miracles wrought miracles, for none is greater than the other, the chosen are known for the chosen know; and therefore them that dare to be with like masters dare to will, and dare the law.

Be silent of the flesh, be silent in graves, be

silent all fools who dare not; for wisdom will enter the heart while being of the heart. Under the spell physical strength is childish when confronting temptation; all shall come to an end, yet you hold the keys of Fate, of authority, and if you take those that weigh down the mightiest of shoulders you shall fall at once to the bottomless pit; your enemies and their like, the silent fools, are subjected by nature to conditions capable of creating sublime sentiments in you; appetites in you; absolute devotion in you- fall not once more into perverseness from that which knows no end, and withal which you will suffer no end.

Be one of those that rebel; and end in rebellion. Be inseparable from love, but love must be reciprocated, so that jealousy may endure only in this; to destroy as egotistical fanaticism. Be of the world; of the spirit; of vengeance; of goodness; of sin; of serpents; of rebellion; be confined; be sterile; be of the fire; be of the fragrance of the truth; be of the gathered select; be travailed- or be silent and rise. As the sun does rise in each morning song; listen to the spirit as the sun rises, and be merciful to those who depend on you for help and listen to petitions and prayers and take charge of every power; and in so doing chase out every Satan from among those who are to inherit everlasting life. Be wise, Angels of name- depart!

Flings

"This time its going to be different." This is what I thought as I sat at my best friend's house staring at the posters on his wall. This guy always had a way to really create a great atmosphere around his place. I can't even remember what the poster was of but it was something really cool about drinking and women.

We were sitting around making jokes and sharing stories about girls when I got a call from one of my Ex's friends. She was super- hot and really sweet, so her phone call really got me excited. From what I could tell from her call she was just bored, and since we had never slept together, I was surprised when she wanted me to come over to her place. I was in automatically, but later realized I was only degrading the value of myself by answering to her every whim.

By de-valuing myself I mean I was going in to a set of circumstances that were not prime to pick her up. If we had been somewhere together and she wanted me to leave with her, this would have been fine, but its not what was happening.

I asked my best friend John, owner of the house we were at, if he wanted to go and visit Meg, the girl who called, and her roommate, and he was not into it. I had to do some real convincing, which was easy because talking to my guy friends is simple, so eventually he decided to come along.

At the girls apartment things went downhill fast. No action whatsoever was going down in my department, but John was into the roommate and made his move by going into her bedroom- leaving me alone with Meg. We sat there with hardly anything to say and the awkward silence was stinging. We really had nothing to talk about because we were both in boredom mode, that's why to this day I simply refuse to go on house calls to girls who are just hanging out.

There's a much better way to approach a woman who wants your company, and this way actually leads to sex on behalf of the man daring enough to try. The trick is to get the girl to do something, anything. The basic principle behind this is that she's not just sitting around, but instead has some momentum behind her.

I thought the right move was going to be to get her to her bedroom, but this was a huge mistake. Once we went to her bedroom the only change was that now she was laying on her back talking and I was sitting on the floor, or the corner of the bed, listening to her problems. I was doing better with myself in the living room than I did in the bedroom, but then again the old saying 'out of the frying pan into the fire' was started for a reason.

At this point I couldn't decide what to do so after listening to her problems for half an hour I suggested we see what John was into. He was waiting for us on the sofa of the front room, but Meg's roommate was still lying in bed, apparently in the same mode as her BFF. This is when it came to me to try to build positive momentum and get the girls excited. I had no help from John because he had went straight for the goods back in this girls room, and when she backed him off he got characteristically upset and sat his ass in the living room alone.

I took in John's story with a little bit of pity because he was a self-proclaimed pick up artist, who had great success in the bars and clubs near his house. I couldn't feel too sorry for him as he went into the girl's kitchen and produced a cold beer from the fridge. He suggested we all drink a few and then risk the D.U.I. we might get in driving back to his place. He believed that by getting the girls into his territory he could get them to do anything he liked.

I thought better of his plan and suggested that Meg grab her roommate from her room, before John tried making his move again. Meg retrieved her friend and while they both gave John some of the coldest stares I have ever seen as he stood leaning over the kitchen counter drinking his beer. I told John to hang out and finish off a few more beers while I took the ladies for a walk.

It was the change of atmosphere that they needed- no more distress, no more idle minds, no more problems, and no more John. We found a Pair of swing-sets around back of the girls' apartment complex, and we actually enjoyed using them, taking turns pushing each other. When we had finally cleared our minds and were living in the present, just enjoying each other's company things changed on the spot.

We all became less like animal predators trying to scare each other off, and we became more intimate with each other like we really were friends for life. We went back in to see where John had ended up, and he was about a beer away from passing out on the girl's sofa, he was drowning in self-pity.

The girls and I hardly even noticed the slurs that came out of him as we passed by him to Meg's bedroom where we could all three of us spend some time. And that was it- we brought the positive attitudes with us into the bedroom and ended up having sex until 3 in the morning.

That's right I got the goods and didn't try any of the patented pick up artist moves that John swears by to this day, as he fills his apartment with trophy after trophy from his last night's conquest. I chose to keep my self- motivated and attentive to the women around me and now I have no problem getting sex whenever I want it.

Recap
1. Momentum- You have to have it before sex. Momentum is like Viagra, only its 100% natural. You need a girl to not just be sitting around half the day before she decides to call you for some action. The wrong way to build momentum is to tire the girl out, doing too much. I tired girl isn't a fun girl, unless she's younger than you, because than she likely has more energy than

after you wear out.

Good momentum starts like an hour before the prime time to get her to have sex with you. An hour is enough time for you to get ready for work, to get ready for the big game on T.V., or to unwind after dinner. The momentum you need to build does not come from her watching t.v. all day. If she calls you from her sofa wanting to talk or hang out because she's been stuck to the sofa all day and she's tired of reruns, this is not good.

After a woman has a completely lazy day she is full of bad energy, she's just been building up a bad negative ball of emotion all day, and now she wants to share that with you. If she chose you to be the one to share all her inner turmoil with, you should definitely reassess the situation, because that energy turned to sex is not the kind of sex you want.

2. Atmosphere is something you create. Its not something you should be afraid of, and it is totally under your control, unlike people.

To really get what it means to create atmosphere you need to leave your preconceived notions at the door. Atmosphere doesn't have to be preplanned or set up in your living room, kitchen, or bathroom. It doesn't exist in a restaurant or in the club, as a matter of fact it doesn't exist. And running around looking for it is a mistake- only if you can't find it. Its not really inside you, but that's a good guess too.

All it takes to create positive feelings about a place is an open attitude. Its a lot like the saying 'you can't see the forest through the trees." In the same way its like going into a flower garden and after examining every single flower leaving to see the other gardens in the area without, you guessed 'stopping to smell the roses." The secret is to look at the whole and stay focused on the individual, only not the individuals that make up the whole, but the individual you are- or who your lover is.

3. Keep yourself clean! This means a lot in the real world. A clean person is one who does not allow the clutter in life to fill his rooms or his mind. I cannot stress it enough that living in a way that reflects inner harmony creates situations in the real world that are harmonious. Getting angry, or overly self- confident are two of the biggest mistakes a pick- up artist can make. They lead to trouble and can easily be avoided by a discriminating person.

What it takes to pick up a beautiful woman is an art, a pick up artist needs to know complete mastery over his actions and his surroundings at all times. This is the only true way to make a women believe they are wanted. You can practice for hours picking up women, but never really understand what it means. If your scoring with the girls its because you have mastered something, but what you master is a part of you- it is you.

Drama 201

So, in order to love a woman, or to be her lover, what it really takes is for you to first love yourself. I hear people all the time telling me that they can't love themselves, but then turn around and pick up a woman that feels the same way about themselves. If you really want to hear something messed up then listen to this. The man who picks up the girl that is like him is locked into that relationship, and they deserve each other.

The art of the pickup is to pick- up the girls that are out of your league, or at least the ones you believe to be so. It takes a real dummy to not see that he has learned the wrong material after his relationships end one after another after another. You need to realize that by being a better person you really are offering what every woman wants. You are tapping into the psyche of all women when you become a pick up artist with skills.

By letting women revolve around you and your plans of action you are in essence inviting women to sleep with you, just for fun. And women love to do this as long as there is no detriment to their selves. The way to ensure no harm is done is to tap deep into her inner desire for an alpha male, and then to create the environment in which you are that male.

When you do this to a woman the woman automatically senses that there are no real strings attached outside of the agreement that you share together. And there isn't either, its all it takes. Be the real world player with class, and create worlds in which her psyche can find fulfillment then you will receive sexual fulfillment together. Its kind of like visiting a fantasy suite in a hotel- without paying the bill.

You are the one that can create this magic world for her, and she will come to you for it. Not only that but remember how I promised that women that are complete strangers to you will flock to you, well this is why, and this is a powerful technique almost entirely overlooked by 99% of pick up artists too busy with their selves and their conquests back at the social bar, or club.

Ch. 2 Notes

Ps. 1-17 in its entirety; Grace, chen, zeker, euprepeia; Intamacy, ahab, philagathos, philoxenos; Accessibility, aman, batah, peitho; Authenticity, emeth, quwm, pistou; Living Light;

De. 18:14-17; Ex. 20:3-17; De. 28; Ez. 24-Set on a pot*, 24:8, 24:16 Son of Man*; Re. 6-8;

Special Thanks to E. L. For the 4ht through the 7th seals; Virtue; arete/dunamis; Lu. 14:16; 1 Pe. 3:2; Pr. 31:30; Lu. 6:19; Ac. 19:11; Jn. 15:17, 17:24; Ph. 2:13; Ro. 5:7; 1 Co 6:1;

Keep Silent; Zec. 2:13; Ps. 31:17; Fools; Pr. 1:7, 10:21; Ps. 107:17; Ec. 5:4; 1 Co. 4:10; Ep. 5:15

Sampson; Jud. 14:1-3, 16:1-4, 15:4,11-14, 16:3-15,30; Keys; Kleis; Is. 22:22; Re. 9:1; Silence; Animals;

Perversions; Pr. 11:3; Eze. 9:9; Mt. 17:17; Ambassadors; Nu. 20:14; Eze. 17:15; Jealousy;

Archangels; Enoch 20:1; Uriel; Raphael; Ruel; Michael; Sariel; Gabriel; Remiel; Silence;

Descent of Angels; Enoch 39:1; Enoch 40:3; Four Angels, Four Voices; Desent of Wisdom and Iniquality; En. 42:1-3; En. 64:2, 70:1-2

CHAPTER THREE
An Impaired Love

A man threw a huge party: he invited all his friends and enemies alike; of all of whom were invited, none showed up for the party. Then the house being angry, the master said into the streets, "Bring in the poor, the lame, the abandoned, and the blind from the highways and hedges." He said to them to come in; for he said that of all who were invited none shall taste of his liquor or food. Then the poor were the guests from that time on at great parties; not the friends and enemies alike, lest they should have to fight and bicker; and ruin the night- so will you be blessed, for the poor and strange will not always seek compensation. Again, for they will have compensation at the resurrection of the just.

The wrestling of those rich men for compensation is preordained; therefore like magicians they use their names to cast spells and draw together crowds; none of these men claims to be innocent or pure, yet each will protest the claims and magic of another of them that has through immodesty become a powerful voice in his part. Like a handful of clay the Giant works the serpents of his hand, and boxes and fights for sport; his works come like rain, like a rain of arrows; he seeks to rule the night and the party. And each Giant claims to be made of the clay of God; he pretends to furnish the flowers with youth; his words come as notes from a flute or shrill pipe. Still his claims of warmth and his magnetic seal spread throughout the night; and still might one, just one of the poor people of the night come in in no embrace, and stand with clasped hands together in salute to all the Giants.

Like an Iason come to cure the ills that fall upon the feet of man, from the troubled course of life. This Iason comes to slaughter the pride of the idolatrous feast; he shall do this in sign and signal; he will wash away the mud of the sea stirred up by the giant beast. He turns the walls of the house to watch the spirits that haunt it; for none invited will taste of the liquor and bread. Iason shall dominate the unseen, the invisible, with his solitary, sterile place in this company; he shall remind those who seek to rule of the work to which Giants belong. Back into the fire he pushes his comrades. He shall be the first, as he was the last; with a sharp stick he shall spit hostile sayings at each Giant, and he will club them over and over and over, he will club the heads of this lost tribe.

Iason will speak with oiled splendor into, unto and of the dusky hue of night; he will unleash horses to run through the streets in the night. His counsels and words give high advice in secret places to the Giants; making them to disappear; them the scum of the pot, to go over the sides because of their mutual clouds of superiority- they go over and into the light as if it were made day.

The meditations of the poor are but musings over the lot of their fallen brothers; those trampled by the Giants; the poor reflect on the universe and sigh. They hear triumphal shouts made by Iason, and they draw near and into his house to receive victory; to be at the resurrection of the just. Like a rock or bone they have come to be saved in the downfall; a new company, anew society, a new magic spell. They will increase in their discerning, in wisdom, in success- or will they first disown the world, the vain world from which they came; left in ruin and depravity. They the new breed will come out of the sea of hate and see the fire (dithalossos). Now there reflection is refined in this new fire; their eyes clarified- this society is false and formed into one great image. A stone column in likeness to the Giant; but this stone is temporal, temporary without possessions to secure, or seize, their hearts and attention; to pull at them like the wealth of their occupancy or to hold them back.

These passionate jewels come to experience the night; Iason affecting their every action; Iason giving hem of the food to eat, and the family to share- the intelligent Giants of the night are this poor lot and all their senses are poured short, with little time their bowels are emptied- their wills acquiesced; opinions obtained to secure acquisition of the stars. These are the Stars that cause the Giants to be lunatics in the night; the vows of the Stars are promised to time alone. In this love feast Iason instructs warning and admonition to the souls of the poor and the noble; like brambles of the hedge or arrows sent to punish and seek revenge for punishment by tyrants; they seek death; these Stars seek death; extremity- death.

They only flower for a time in the night. Seeing them here, I came into this house and party in the night and Iason brought me into the courtyard in which was the gate and three sides round-about a fence; inside which was the garden, and over which stood the house at one far end with its great windows, arches, posts, and seven steps. At three in the morning I saw a great tree there standing in the courtyard with its shadow shrouding a portion of the yard, and its high stature; beneath the great tree was a pool of water which fed the tree and made it tall; yet none of the trees on either side of the courtyard was of so great a stature as the tree next the waters, for that one tree did restrain them all, and caused the field to faint around it.

At six that morning I saw there in the courtyard the likeness of fire consume the yard and all its ornaments, and then my spirit lifted me up as I looked toward the image of what lie inside the gated yard- that one great house- and I entered into the house- and saw every wicked form of nature and of man, idols all around me on the walls. In my arrogance and elation I felt a high pride swell in my self- confidence; like a crystal image I saw myself consumed and my mind turned off leaving my body but a sage genius of the night.

Relationships

"Sometimes I wish there were three of me." This is what I sometimes think about, but I'm pretty sure a lot of the time that three wouldn't be enough of me. Realistically though one is enough of me, just so long as I can pick up beautiful women, whom will do most of the work.

The first time I met Josie I was working my ass off as usual trying to work my way through college. She was gorgeous and tall, she was it. I had been working at this place near my college campus for almost a year when she got on and I found out she was trying to do the same thing.

I was top of my class at school, but that didn't get me any breaks at work. I worked hard every day with some real work-ethic (that is until Josie started working with me.) I immediately saw the attention she received at work, and I knew that if I landed her with some quality pick up material I could make life a lot easier for the both of us.

The key to working with her was that no matter what she did she always got a break, this included time to talk to guys and boyfriends while she was on the clock. I never got away with slacking off on the clock, so I figured with a little effort I get Josie back to work, only now she'd be doing most of my work.

The boss didn't care what she did, she was too good looking, and I began to talk to her and show her the ropes at work. Giving her the impression that my job was great and that I was really good at it, and hard-working, was easy because all I had to do was watch out for her to start to slack off and talk to other guys and then I would immediately concentrate on whatever it was I was doing only way more hardcore than the task required.

By my concentrating on what I was doing I was actually giving off the impression that I was having more fun than anyone else. The next time I spoke to Josie, and she was slacking off a little before the end of the day, all I had to do was ask her for a little help at what I was doing to get out of there. She liked talking to me already, and now she had a reason to get physical, which is a good thing- Kino!

Anyway, those late night work sessions escalated pretty quickly and before long she was coming home with me and we were having great sex! The effort I put into showing her things at work paid off double when she now used her spare time at work in doing the tasks I hated doing, and she almost never spoke to other guys anymore because she was too busy.

The first time I met Ness I was stunned. She was the average sorority girl, but in most of my classes sorority life was the biggest secret since Socrates. She was smart and beautiful, but she was way to quiet. None of the guys in our classes at the college new how to approach her, so she seemed very untouchable.

The only reason she even knew I existed was I was very vocal in my classes and I liked to help other classmates when I had a chance. Ness didn't need help though because she was straight A material, the only way to approach her was to wait, which is a strong point of mine- patience.

After our classes really started to move along in the materials we were responsible for I didn't have much time to fantasize about what it would be like to pick up on Ness, so I did what I did best- I focused on the task at hand, which happened to be getting an insane amount of paperwork turned in.

I needed a way to get the smartest and prettiest girl in class to liven up a bit so these classes would be bearable, so I decided to put in some extra time after class. Gathering my papers and hanging around after class was dismissed was a good move because it reminded me that I wasn't the only one falling behind.

I quickly moved this taking of a few extra minutes after class to my creating an encounter with Ness. She never hung around after class, but at least I could see which way she was going. I approached her in the same fashion as most beautiful women and didn't even give her a chance to act shy. I used my efforts to make myself look like the cool kid come apart. I shuffled papers as I walked next to her, but as soon as she noticed this I cut the act and concentrated my effort, which had the effect of quickly assembling my papers while moving at her pace, side- by- side with her step. I came together in front of her and she was amazed; she saw what she wanted but never took the time to ask for- me.

It was a long walk that day, but it was nice and sunny outside, so taking her time Ness was relaxed as she walked with me. Before long she had opened up about her life and studies. I used this opportunity not only to sleep with the hottest girl in any of my classes, but also my grades improved as soon as Ness was doing most of the homework.

She never questioned doing my classwork because she knew that I was way too focused on my degree to risk anything crazy. I used concentrated effort to show her it was ok to help, and thus be helped- only I helped her sexually.

From that day on I walked home with her and she was doing half of the research I hadn't had time for, but I found the time for her. Concentrated effort sounds so boring and difficult but its really no different than multi-tasking.

Recap

1. Effort- you got to really be there in the moment to know what you are doing. Confidence is a direct result of sustained effort, and confidence attracts attention, especially from women. The saying about 'try, try again." Wasn't meant for losers, it was meant for those people that want more confidence in their daily lives.

Effort is like the moving sky. Sounds strange but hear me out. Effort can't really be trapped up in a bottle, or judged- unless you're referring to energy, but I'm not. What you do with yourself at any given time is what is considered effort. If you put effort into your home life, it gets better at home. If you put effort into your social life, it gets better. So effort isn't any certain thing at all, its just what you do with yourself.

2. Concentration is easier than it sounds. It doesn't have to be like the child's game where you remember pictures. In fact concentration is better left to the individual. It speaks volumes about ones' character, which is another good thing that women love. Showing focus on a task, concentrating, shows that you are the caring sort of person, the person other people want to be around. And no matter how many times you lose your concentration you can easily get it back with a little effort just doing what you always do- do work!

I need to stress again that concentrating is not hard. It does not mean you are remembering facts and trying to recall them with amazing accuracy, as some would define it. But more than that concentrating is the act of slowing down your actions and relying solely on past and learned events and outcomes of a specific function or whole of that specific act. Sounds complicated but its really not, as I'll explain below in the 3 part of this section.

3. An act of love can be defined by its outcome; if it is an act of love than its result must

be a desirable one. You go to the store to buy a t-shirt; you find a shirt you think you really love it, so you buy it. Story ends when you wear that shirt and you feel love: for the shirt, for your buying it, and for everyone who sees you in it because its so cool.

Love should be like a brand, a certain label of fashion. If you were to go out shopping and always but the same label of clothing you would be a model of love. Not only that, but every time you go out as the pickup artist and your wearing your love label, you are essentially letting other people identify with you. Love is never impaired by love itself. You should be wearing a label you love, so that when your life as a pick up artist really picks up momentum you will be identified as a player with game. Sentiment is fashionable, and women will know before and after that you are open for sex if they want it.

Drama 301

It's easy to see how this technique can be easily applied to the pickup artist, and so it should be. Because you have the right to be happy you should never feel bad about your methods. People do these things all the time with zero awareness of what they're doing, so do you but now you can easily apply your time to picking up girls.

Guidelines for this behavior are so minimal they're hardly worth mentioning, but here goes anyway.

-In life a lot of times, especially in the life of a pickup artist, its dog eat dog- as the saying goes. Being the alpha male sometimes means taking things that weren't initially intended for your pleasure. Saying this is easy but keeping it unproven is another matter altogether.

Just because you meet a beautiful woman in a perfect situation doesn't mean that she's completely available to you. That's your job in figuring out just who she is, and how available you can get her to be.

The nonsense of it all is that most men before they become pick up artists are aware of the rejection factor. Well I'm here to tell you not to give any mind to this type of thinking. A rejection from a woman simply means that you are not completely giving her the 'go' to please you. Believe it or not you've got the alpha male in you- its just bigger than you want to admit at times.

You are accessing the girl's desire to please you, and by doing so you are accessing her inner alpha female- that's the way that a woman pleases a man. If you give her any doubt about the situation she doesn't know any better than to trust your instinct- that's how females live. Trust yourself to make responsible decisions and the women will trust you as well.

Therefor a rejection is really just your way of telling a girl that sex could be a mistake at this point, this is why sometimes its just better for the pick-up artist to go for a kiss or even a phone number. You already know this - I'm moving on.

Ch. 3 Notes

The Great Supper; Lu. 14:16; the poor;negation; nepthalim; magicians; chartom; Azoth; Azmon; Atsmown; Azazel; Azarael; Azure; Azzur; Azzuwr; Chaste; Hagnos; Protested; uwd; ne; Gibbowr; rapha; nephiyl; Immanual; hollow; nebab; shoal; Sheqaruwrath; abtiyt; pelos;

Jasiel; Iason; Isreal; pukted; yowreh; yarah; malqowsh; enowsh; tsiyts; huperakmos; mashrowqiy;

Qana; zeloo; chabaq; aspazomai; zabach; chag; eidolothuton; chagag; heorte; dromos; Miracle; owth, semeion; rephesh;

Acar; phulake; authanteo; aoratos; badad; galmuwd; tsiyah; eremos; uriel; rishown; shebet; sharbiyt; rhabdos; Sharia; saray; matteh; maqael; yetshar; shemen; elaion; oreb; cuwc; hippos;

Dobar; melak; cowd; bouleuo; buwz; maac, qalal; anan; en; haguwth; hagiyg; higgayown; siyach; siychah; alaz, rinnah; thriambeuo;

Etsem; Isaih; peter; oume; orechan; bath; cheber; plethos; biya; chakkiym; yakach; sekel; sophos; apeipomen; houto;

Hebel; shau; mataiotos; yam; dithalossos; Refined; zaqaq; tsaraph; matstsebeh; maskiyth;

proskairos; achaz; achuzzah; yereshah; ktema; atsar;pascho; homosopathes; adown; ba'al; kurios; oikodespotes; sekel; aisheteroon;

Neriah; gebuwl; yowm; owd; rega; brachus; chronos; abah; thelo; gnome; yaba; nephesh; Obtaineth; puwq; peripoiesis; kowkab; aster; astron; Lunatick;

Neder; nadar; euche; zeman; mowed; malach; artuo; kairos; agape;muwear; mocar; paideia; nephesh; psuche; nediybah; ceneh; batos; ben; chets; chitstsiy; naqam; dike; orge; tyrannus; turannos; eschato; teleute; mowth;

Ez. 40:17-27

Ez. 31

Ez 8:1

Teraphim; Pride; geah; gobahh; alazoneia

Cupidity; zekuwkiyth; kowc; teraphiym; eidololatreia; kateidolos; baar; malak; phroneo; cuwr; ma'aleh;

Re. 13-15:2 Special thanks to E.L.; samaon; Samael,salt, sulpher, mercury.

CHAPTER FOUR
An Impaired Love

I came to the place you chose out of all
places; and I learned your name, it was your name
that I sought in this place in which we have come
to be. Not forgetting the name of myself and
yourself, as some may do; but instead we sat
exhorting one another; and happy we became as
we saw the day approaching; as if to learn some
great lesson instructed to us by the morning sun.
Draw me, we will run after thee; and be glad and
rejoice in each other- we will remember the love
more than the wine- to which we attend; listening
close, listening smartly together; witnessing
rumors and reports sounding near our ears; pouring
from the lips of whomsoever tells- themselves
utterly oblivious.

None can come to me, but through you;
through your name I will draw all men to me. But
rather I am not a child, for I will go to all who send
you and your name will I speak; I will speak of no
evil, and of no angst- but rather gentle and meek

will I speak to all, for the tongue is a fire among our members; of all our body the tongue does set fire the course of nature, name, and self. My self keeps the fire, the silence, and the love for I refrain my tongue and lips from evil, and let no evil enter me by your name. Your speech is of grace, and you answer every man as you should- for many things will offend all, but you offend not in your word; so save me and make me perfect in mind and body.

A word, matter, course is to speak and to subdue to commune with the noise- and to me it makes me to hum aloud in the uproar you rush at me with sounds; sounds like rain and wind; sounds instructing me to discourse; to glean your words and collect the bounty of your lips- In force, but without arguing reproves, but pleasant words likened to honeycombs, sweet souls, and good health- yes, with words like apples of gold in pictures of silver.

I tell the truth- so shall I be an enemy among those who affect you well but would exclude you so you might affect them? I thought on your words and turned my feet- I say and testify your word moved me to walk, but not vainly. I consider the work of your fingers, and the moon and stars, I consider your way, and consider the lilies of the field- they grow but toil not neither spin- let this meditation be wholly given over to you. I am given wholly to see you prosper in the sight of all, so that as they think on you and I we may mark this time together to commemorate and remind us of all the rewards, not the punishments; I may mention the way my heart is hot within me as I muse the fire of your tongue. Make me to remember to be with you in spirit, and I shall do the same for you in life, spirit, and peace- for as we think we are, thus we are.

Despite how they suffer for us in the fire, we too must be wise and of the same mind, for their feet run to evil and are soon to shed blood; so may our hearts devise no wicked images, but may our feet move swift and run not to evil; even so may our work provide fruit of good labors, so we may but hold out until the rising stars replace the morning star. Our zeal will consume our enemies, as they are prone to forget.

I will return to you and show you great things which you have done, you and your way; great thing throughout; the breastplate and helmet of you that sent me and to you to which I came. A performance of miraculous execution and of force and power by way of my possessions; to accomplish what time has not; to emulate the harvest of the weak if I am weak; and to all virtues used might I save but some by you.

You say to me there is time yet, and I say to you to look to the fields for the time is now. I only mean that by emulation of my body, your body may trust it is heart, and walk in my ways. Sure, as we look about us we may see some who despise us, for some are to die; but to show the work of our heart, you and I, we may affect their conscience as witnesses, meanwhile their thoughts are tied in accusing or excusing one another.

Like thieves stealing jewels and handing them out to the poor is our unconscious breath; makers of habit practicing our walk on their hearts, but in truth we tread paths on our own hearts-bearing witness to one another in secret knowledge of one to the other in places they can't go, for they at this hour take the offerings of others and other conscience and are made weak by it. Still by doing so the weak will multiply and we may save but some of them- and of all things whatever we ask them some shall do and rejoice.

Abide in me, and let my words abide in you-then whatever we ask will be done, and we may sing praises as one breathing creature, or as one body of vitality does. With great height and refreshing winds we shall shake and wrestle like spirit and mind; we will be beautiful, as we have come to be at home with one another- knowing the conjurations of refusal from them that know. We become circumspect and evening and morning become one voice; one voice of fire hating every false way- for from our mouths comes knowledge and light as a candle enlightening the darkness, the poor, the deceitful; all together- we lighten all their eyes. They are a generation, a nation, and a people that they should show praise of us, and to call upon us like from out of the darkness and into the light.

Our successes are well indicated to us, and others are well-reverent to this; as we comprehend the exercising of our sentiments, the onlookers like beasts still held under bit and bridle, and still knowing they can't come near to us. We have tilled our lands and became satisfied; we do not follow vanity nor void. We pass lifetimes in the present; awakened by our livelihoods and spending existence in the home of our friend, still telling them of great things to come and of those that have passed. We expecting no compensation for we lack no message, nor have we from the beginning from which we loved one another, and walked honestly toward them that are without- and now we lack nothing, nor lack anything that pertains to life and being; alive, of the flesh, and strong.

A maxim meant to revive the conversation of any that come near enough to hear, or have been absent of our affairs- I stand fast and strive in spirit and mind with faith like an army of peace adjured by the living, Christ.

Well...

Now you know. You know the secrets to becoming a perfect lover. Its so simple is crazy, but so is love. There is nothing you can't do by following the instructions contained in this book, and there likely won't be any changing this for some time. The stuff that matters is in having fun while you become not just another pick up artist. Bad attitudes don't make this stuff not work, bad attitudes just make this life different. You can in theory be the worst person, and still get away with being the best possible lover, I've seen it before. What counts is that you are capable of being different and still able to apply this material.

Everyone is different, and I don't expect anyone to be just like me, or to use these methods as I did. You can just do it your way, but the principles of it will still be available to you, no matter what your like or what you're in to. This book is made to transcend race lines, cross borders, be timeless, and its best to follow any information contained within this book with your gut.

Don't forget that living with game means living to its fullest, which means you can't skip out on the other facets of your life. If you start to think that life is just a game than your game will fall apart. You have to understand that the methods, techniques, and results of the pick-up artist are so real that everyone needs to try them once in life just to be fully alive- its human nature.

AIL

As you try more and more of the techniques herein you may find yourself looking for more information, so if that becomes the case the best advice I can give is that I have also written a short series of novels that, while they are not instructional in nature as this material is, they are formatted to be essential living tools. By living tools I mean that the characters and situations contained in the novels are not to be found elsewhere in any other media you may come across. These novels are unique and completely distinct from the secular culture in which the average pick up artist was raised and now thrives, so if you feel the need then go ahead and try them out.

The series name is "An Impaired Love" and can be found online. The materials within them are construed to develop habits exactly similar to the instructional tips found here, but they are formatted to read just as if you were involved in reading any story. Albeit, in writing these novels I put my best foot forward and designed them to have positive lasting impact in the readers' life, often without any cognizance on the reader's part. They're just made for the little voice of conscience that is said to exist. The precept behind them is entirely revolutionary, much like the think and blink tactics of this book, but it's harder to explain how to write a novel that is intended to be read as a manual than I care to admit.

There are doubtless other, and by point of view better, books on PUAs, but the other books by the more professional artists out there have not one single gain on you than you already have-except experience, which this book is full of to the top. The methods are the same to a degree, its just up to you to find your own program and to work it from there- this is just to get you moving remember!

Why love works!

Love works in mysterious ways. Have you ever heard that? Well it's true, but what does it mean. To me it has always meant that love works where the eyes can't see. Before you close your eyes and wait for love though, I'd like to offer these alternative approaches:

Love comes when least expected.

Love is a battlefield.

Love is never impaired by love.

It's the third option that I want to focus on- Love is never impaired by love.

For this to be true that must mean that love, any love, is just as strong as the next. The girl of your dreams, if this holds true, might just as well be replaced by the girl next door. The key is your letting it happen. Allowing love to open fully and explain the secrets of your heart is no easy trick, but with patients it can happen.

I'm not really a mushy or completely over-sensitive person, I'm actually quite aggressive, which is something I'm working on especially in staying patient. But the point is, that love works on whoever it wants in its own special way. There is no love potion, no secret recipe that is all defining. Only are there different ways of viewing the world. If you want to see the world one way, than do it, but it's essential for good game, or being the perfect lover, that you are able to shift gears, or may I call it being open to change.

The only material not presented in this book, in order to keep to its short format and length are on everyday living. But you're already a living breathing person who understands the problems that men and women face in the world today, so I have decided to leave out my own personal experiences.

Accurate portrayal of true love is more difficult than I ever imagined, it's just out there.

Ch. 4 Notes

Qashab; qesheb; qashshub; shama; shema; shoma; shama; shemets; shimtsah ekkremamai; eklaleo; eklanthanomai;

Dabar; hemyah; hamah; hamuwllah; leqach; laqat; laqaq; milleh; millah;

Zakar; zeker; zakar; mimnesko; mnaomai; mneme; mnemoneuo;

Alilah; aliyliyah; chayli; masay; maaseh;asah;

Colam; cela; epautophoro; auto; aer; phor; paal; poal;

Nephesh; nepheth; nopheth; naphash; naphtuwl; ruwach; na; na'ah; ca'ar; cearah; phronema; phronesis; phronimos; phrontizo; anamartetos; anameno; ananepho; anantirrhetos; anastasis; sophroneo; sophronizo; sophronismos; hupomeno; hupomimnesko; hupomone; hupopleo;

Biyn; biyneh; biynah; biyrah; yada; yeda; yidde'oniy; yahh; ginosko; ginomai; sakal; sekel; eusemos; eusebos; eusebes; noeo; phroneo

Diego; diagregoreo; bios; bioo; biotikos; chay; choy; chaya; chiydah; cheya; cheyva;

De. 12:5; He. 10:25; Seven; Song 1:4; Jn. 6:44; Jn. 12:32

Je. 1:7; Tit. 3:2; Ja. 3:6; Pr. 13:3; Pe. 3:10; Mt. 5:37; Col. 4:6; Ja. 3:2; Jb. 6:25; Pr. 16:24, 25:11; Ga. 4:16-7;

Ps. 49:59; Ep. 4:17; Ps. 8; Hag. 1:5; Mt 6:28; Ps. 19:14; 1 Ti. 4:15; Ps. 39:3; Ro. 8:6; Pe. 4:1;

Pr. 1:16, 6:18; Ne. 4:21;Ps. 119:139; Lu 8:39; Is. 59:17; Jn. 4:34, 9:4, 4:35; Ro. 11:14; 1 Co 9:22;

Pr. 28:26; Lu. 18:19; Jud. 13:22; Ro. 2:15, 9:1; 1 Co. 8:7

Effort; Ac. 13:42; Mt. 21:22; Jn. 15:7; Ac 16:15; Ja. 5:18; Ps. 55:17

Ps. 119:104, 18:28, 32:9; Pr. 2:6, 29:13, 12:11; Pe. 2:9;

Mk. 5:19; Pe. 11:13; Th. 4:12; Ph. 1:27; S. 17:26; Mt. 26:63;

www.ingramcontent.com/pod-product-compliance
Lightning Source LLC
Chambersburg PA
CBHW020518030426
42337CB00011B/453